THE OCD
TREATMENT
JOURNAL

Independently Published: Fairfax, VA

ISBN: 979-8-9870037-7-0

Printed in the United States of America
Unless otherwise noted, scriptural references are taken from the English Standard Version.

ESV Study Bible: English Standard Version. Crossway Bibles; 2008.

Note: This journal is intended to provide easy access to resources but is not medical advice and does not act as a substitute for proper care. OCD is best treated in coordination with counselors/psychologists and medical providers such as psychiatric specialists and general practitioners. This journal is best used in coordination with your treatment team.

The OCD Treatment Journal: A Faith-Based Guide to
Understanding and Treating Obsessive Compulsive Disorder

Note From the Author

In school, they taught that Obsessive Compulsive Disorder (OCD) had one of the simplest diagnostic criteria in the *Diagnostic and Statistical Manual of Mental Disorders (DSM)*. The *DSM*, or "Bible of Psychiatry/Psychology," provides a framework for understanding mental health and is the attempt of a panel of experts to organize mental malady into categories. While other specialties of medicine utilize blood tests and scans, mental health providers rely on identifying patterns of signs and symptoms to make diagnoses. Patients often feel confined to a "box" as they read the criteria presented within any of the *DSM*'s categories. We will explore this criterion later.

The "simple" criteria for diagnosing OCD in no way reflect the potential for serious functional impairment in the lives of those who suffer. I have seen this firsthand. What takes less than a page to describe in the *DSM* may be the cause of lost jobs or relationships, difficulties in school, and physical health concerns, among other impacts.

It is an understatement to say that humans are complex; this is no more apparent than in our neurophysiology and no more mysterious than in the interactions between the brain and what we call the "mind". The early part of the 21st century has witnessed a shift toward a biological model of understanding psychiatry. Researchers have focused efforts on understanding how psychological disorders may be manifestations of neurologic abnormality or how aberrant neurotransmitters, genetics, and epigenetic factors may result in the symptoms we observe in patients. Some of these theories we will explore in this journal. Yet, while biopsychology has made great advancements, we remember that psychiatry is the field of the space between the physical and the nonphysical, and we must hold that space with an open hand. Humans are to be understood not only in light of our biology, but also in the context of our relationships, upbringing, behavior, habits, thinking, and beliefs, among many other factors. The future of psychological research may provide surprising insights into the etiology (causes), pathophysiology (processes of disease), and treatment of OCD, biologic or otherwise.

This journal, then, stands in the space between simple diagnostic criteria and potentially serious functional impairment, between physical factors such as neurobiology and anatomy, and nonphysical elements like thought patterns and habits. Its goal is to both educate and, through that education, to empower you to fight back against OCD.

Working with patients who have OCD has been one of the most rewarding aspects of my career. As it is effectively treated, the freedom experienced is profound. The brain with OCD is a powerful processor that craves something to process; when it is freed from the shackles of obsessive thoughts and ruminating behavior, that energy can be poured into countless fruitful endeavors.

I wish you all the best in your pursuit of mental wellness.

Warmly,

Adam O'Neill, PA-C, DMSc

Psychiatry

Diagnostic and Statistical Manual of Mental Disorders

The concept of diagnostic labels in psychiatry can be a source of controversy. Because there are no blood or imaging tests (at least not yet) that can provide an exact diagnosis, we base our diagnoses on observable and reported thoughts and behavior. I have seen labels do significant harm to patients. Labels carry connotations and may be fraught with public misinformation that could discourage a patient from healing. I have also seen labels be of great help to patients. This has been especially true in OCD. The patient who presents for the first time with OCD may, but often hasn't, identified their symptoms as a part of the disorder. Instead, they may feel as though they are "going crazy" or "losing their mind." Depending on the content of their intrusive thoughts, they may feel they are a "sexual deviant", "predator", "apostate", "psychopath", among many other attempts to understand why they are having the particular thoughts they are having.

In the moments between hearing their story and delivering the diagnosis, my heart breaks. As the picture becomes clearer, from within me comes the desire to stop their distress, "you aren't going crazy, you aren't a predator, this is OCD, and it's going to be okay!". I've seen tangible peace wash over a patient when they realize they aren't the many things their mind has been telling them. It's a moment I cherish. Then the real work begins. Just as quickly as that peace has come over them, their mind accuses them again. So we must begin the work of treating OCD at its source.

First, however, let's examine the diagnostic criteria for the disorder as taken from the Fifth Edition of the *Diagnostic and Statistical Manual of Mental Disorders*:

A. Presence of obsessions, compulsions, or both:

Obsessions are defined by (1) and (2):

1. Recurrent and persistent thoughts, urges, or images that are experienced, at some time during the disturbance, as intrusive and unwanted, and that in most individuals cause marked anxiety or distress.

2. The individual attempts to ignore or suppress such thoughts, urges, or images, or to neutralize them with some other thought or action (i.e., by performing a compulsion).

Compulsions are defined by (1) and (2):

1. Repetitive behaviors (e.g., hand washing, ordering, checking) or mental acts (e.g., praying, counting, repeating words silently) that the individual feels driven to perform in response to an obsession or according to rules that must be applied rigidly.

2. The behaviors or mental acts are aimed at preventing or reducing anxiety or distress, or preventing some dreaded event or situation; however, these behaviors or mental acts are not connected in a realistic way with what they are designed to neutralize or prevent, or are clearly excessive.

Note: Young children may not be able to articulate the aims of these behaviors or mental acts.

B. The obsessions or compulsions are time-consuming (e.g., take more than 1 hour per day) or cause clinically significant distress or impairment in social, occupational, or other important areas of functioning.

C. The obsessive-compulsive symptoms are not attributable to the physiological effects of a substance (e.g., a drug of abuse, a medication) or another medical condition.

D. The disturbance is not better explained by the symptoms of another mental disorder (e.g., excessive worries, as in generalized anxiety disorder; preoccupation with appearance, as in body dysmorphic disorder; difficulty discarding or parting with possessions, as in hoarding disorder; hair pulling, as in trichotillomania [hair-pulling disorder]; skin picking, as in excoriation [skin-picking] disorder; stereotypies, as in stereotypic movement disorder; ritualized eating behavior, as in eating disorders; preoccupation with substances or gambling, as in substance-related and addictive disorders; preoccupation with having an illness, as in illness anxiety disorder; sexual urges or fantasies, as in paraphilic disorders; impulses, as in disruptive, impulse-control, and conduct disorders; guilty ruminations, as in major depressive disorder; thought insertion or delusional preoccupations, as in schizophrenia spectrum and other psychotic disorders; or repetitive patterns of behavior, as in autism spectrum disorder).

To make the diagnosis, patients must meet the criteria outlined in A, B, C, and D. Criteria A is the presence of Obsessions or Compulsions. Nearly everyone experiences occasional thoughts that share similarities with those experienced by patients with OCD; what differs is the emotional value or weight placed on those thoughts. Whereas someone without OCD may shrug off an odd, gruesome, or unpleasant thought, patients with OCD associate having the *thought* with having an *intention* or even with having completed the *action* itself. This is defined as "cognitive misattribution".

Compulsions may include behavioral rituals that an independent observer can see (such as hand washing or checking) or they may be mental acts or rituals. The mental rituals are often missed because they aren't observable to an outside viewer. I have been asked many times what qualifies as a mental ritual. Generally, if there's something you *must* think in order to feel relief from anxiety, and it occurs *repeatedly*, it is likely to be a mental ritual. Some refer to OCD that only presents as obsessional thinking as "Pure O, OCD," though the DSM does not officially recognize that term.

Criteria B ensures that the symptoms are present to a degree that makes them functionally impairing for the patient. Criterion C and D are present to make sure that the diagnosis is not due to a substance (C) which would be a different clinical entity altogether and to make sure that the diagnosis of OCD is the most likely of all the diagnoses listed in the *DSM* and not simply a manifestation of another condition (D) (of which they list some, though not exhaustive).

Finally, the *DSM* provides information for providers to specify:

Specify if:

> **With good or fair insight:** The individual recognizes that obsessive-compulsive disorder beliefs are definitely or probably not true or that they may or may not be true.

> **With poor insight:** The individual thinks obsessive-compulsive disorder beliefs are probably true.

With absent insight/delusional beliefs: The individual is completely convinced that obsessive-compulsive disorder beliefs are true.

Specify if:

Tic-related: The individual has a current or past history of a tic disorder.

Insight in psychiatry is an important component of any assessment. It has been said that there are three components to general insight: (1) knowledge that something is a problem, (2) knowledge of our role within that problem, and (3) knowledge of something we could personally do to address that problem. Within OCD, these components of insight have more to do with whether a patient is able to recognize the thoughts and compulsions *as* OCD rather than as a purely logical and true belief.

The modifier to specify if OCD is occurring alongside Tic Disorder is important and will be discussed alongside other commonly co-occurring and related conditions later.

OCD Subtypes

The criteria listed above speak of obsessions and compulsions very generally, but they can often be broken down further into particular "subtypes". These subtypes aren't outlined in the DSM criteria, though they are listed in the introduction to the OCD chapter. They can provide a helpful framework for understanding what type of OCD someone is experiencing. Some patients with OCD experience multiple subtypes at once, while others may experience only one. It is very common for patients to experience multiple subtypes throughout their life (eg. dealing with cleanliness intrusive thoughts and rituals in childhood and scrupulosity in adulthood).

Here are some of the most common OCD subtypes:

Contamination/Cleaning OCD* – fear of dirt, germs, toxins, etc. Can include the fear that they may be transmitted to a loved one, often including washing or cleaning compulsions.

Scrupulosity OCD – OCD that focuses on morality, faith, and rules. Can include intrusive thoughts about one's faith in God, intrusive blasphemous thoughts, or doubts about salvation or the truthfulness of Scripture. Often includes compulsions such as confessing, praying, and analyzing theology to ensure one believes "sufficiently."

Symmetry or Ordering OCD* – OCD that involves alignment, symmetry, or order of specific objects or people within one's environment. Compulsions may include reorganization, cleaning, or even mental rituals aimed at "evening out" something that feels off.

Checking or Counting OCD – this type of OCD may involve making sure that electronics or appliances are turned off, doors or windows are locked, among other checks. Also included in this category are counting the number or type of objects or people in an environment.

Relational OCD (rOCD) – this lesser-known OCD subcategory involves a patient's relationships with others. They may worry that their significant other is not the right person for them, that they don't love them sufficiently, or that they aren't marriage material. This type of OCD may also include thoughts that a relationship is in turmoil, that someone is mad or upset with them, or that they have offended someone they care about.

Sexual Orientation OCD (SO-OCD) – involves intrusive thoughts that one identifies with a sexual orientation different from the one they currently have. Examples could include that a heterosexual individual is experiencing same-sex attraction because they sat where a same-sex individual sat or looked at them in a certain way.

Harm OCD* – includes intrusive thoughts that harm may come to self or others (often loved ones), either intentionally or unintentionally. Could include fear that being in the presence of something sharp means that one would use that item to hurt someone else.

Forbidden or Taboo Thoughts OCD* – OCD that involves intrusive thoughts and images that are considered repulsive, offensive, illegal, or blasphemous. Patients may worry that these thoughts represent some sort of underlying condition (eg. pedophilia, possession, or Satan worship, psychopathy, etc.).

*Denotes those mentioned explicitly by the *DSM*.

Roots of Certainty and Control

We may explore, if only briefly, the cognitive roots of OCD. As humans living in a dangerous world, our brains have been hardwired to keep us safe. For that reason, two of the biggest causes of fear and anxiety are *uncertainty* and lack of *control.*

The rustling we hear in the bush could be a squirrel, or it could be a tiger, and until our brains determine definitively which it is, we will work to resolve that uncertainty. If we are not able to resolve the uncertainty with action (eg. looking in the bush to see or observing it from another angle), we begin to worry. Worry is an attempt to work through potential scenarios that could cause us harm. The problem is that those scenarios are often unlikely to occur, or they are scenarios we've worked through in the past, and we continue to think about them (this is what we call rumination). It's not likely that from my home in Northern Virginia, a tiger will leap out of a bush; it's much more likely to be a squirrel, yet much of the time we spend worrying is about things just as likely as that absurd example. In addition to resolving uncertainty, there's another element we biologically crave: control. When something is outside of our control, it is perceived as a potential threat.

There are many ways we might try to exert control, but one commonly seen in OCD is avoidance. There's a reason the amygdala (fear center) and hippocampus (memory center) are situated near one another. We want to make sure if something caused us pain in the past, that we encode that into memory and are able to elicit a sufficient fear response and subsequent avoidance if we come into contact with it in the future, so we don't get hurt again. If we do happen to come into contact with it again, we want to *take action*. Having control over the things that scare us helps us feel secure.

So we can see how OCD is fueled by these two components of certainty and control. Much of what leads to OCD loops is a wrestling with some type of uncertainty and illogical attempts to employ compulsions as a form of control (or the form of control we call avoidance). We see in Figure 1 that uncertainty caused by a trigger thought or image leads to anxiety, something feels "not right," and we need to identify the action within our control to fix this feeling. This produces only temporary relief, which is replaced by anxiety when another trigger thought or image occurs.

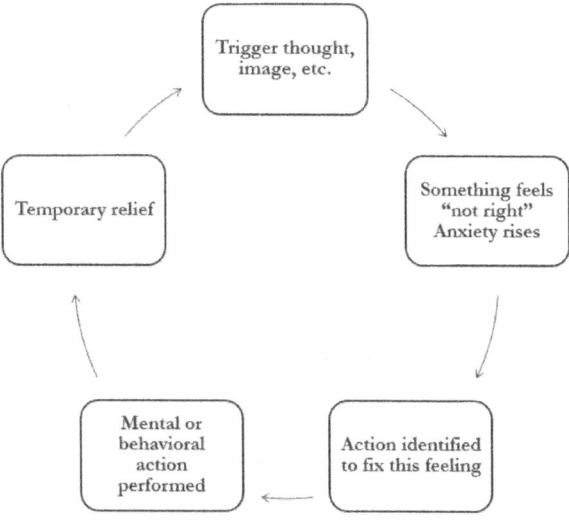

Figure 1. OCD Cognitive Behavioral Loop

Healing comes as we learn to sit in uncertainty without the need to exert control. That's part of what the treatment entails. Exposure and Response Prevention (ERP) is a form of learning to sit within uncertainty and resist attempts to control the situation through compulsion.'

Proposed Neurobiological Model

It is thought that OCD is a manifestation not of problems with one neurotransmitter or region of the brain but of potentially several neurotransmitters and different brain regions connected in particular circuits. The most implicated circuit in OCD today is roughly outlined in Figure 2, known as the Cortico-striato-thalamo-cortical circuit (CSTC), so named for each region in the total circuit. In a specific spot in the outermost region of the brain, called the cortex, lies an area right above the eyes, called the orbitofrontal cortex (OFC). This area, along with the anterior cingulate cortex (ACC), seems to be responsible for alerting us that something is wrong. Think of it as the check engine light in your car alerting you that something needs to be fixed. That region of the brain sends a signal to the deeper parts of the brain in the striatum called the basal ganglia. The basal ganglia has two pathways, the direct and indirect pathways. The direct pathway is responsible for encouraging behaviors, and the indirect pathway is responsible for inhibiting behaviors. Signals from these regions are communicated back to the cortex through our brain's relay station, the thalamus. It's important to note that this pathway is present in everyone, including those without OCD, however in OCD the OFC seems to alert that something is wrong much more frequently and the deep brain sends strong signals from the direct pathway to encourage behavior again and again while sending weak signals from the inhibitory, indirect, pathway. A loop is formed whereby temporary relief from the feeling that something is wrong encourages more of that behavior in the future.

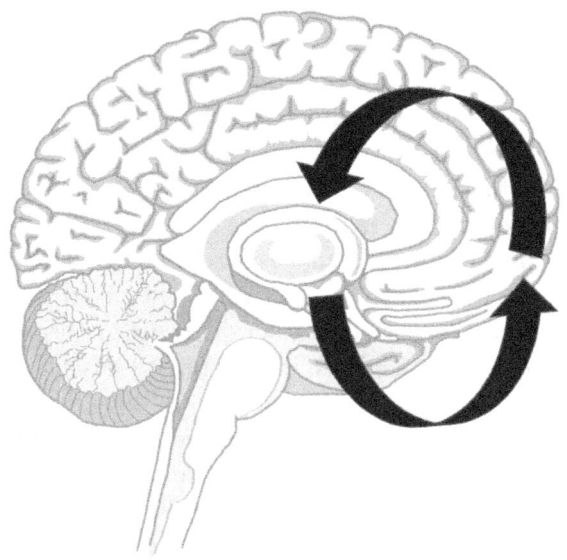

Figure 2. Cortico-striato-thalamo-cortico Circuit (CSTC)

In addition to neuronal circuits, it is believed that neurotransmitters play a role in OCD. Neurons are connected through small spaces where neurotransmitters are released (called the synaptic cleft). As a signal is sent down one neuron, small pockets called vesicles of neurotransmitters fuse with the edge of a neuron to release their contents into this space. The receiving neuron has specialized receptors that receive serotonin, norepinephrine, dopamine, and other neurotransmitters. Once this is done, the signal continues down its intended path. This process happens in milliseconds, a true miracle.

Our bodies conserve extra neurotransmitters by activating a special receptor that reabsorbs them into the sending neuron, allowing them to be used later. Many of the medication interventions in the treatment of OCD function by blocking this reuptake so that the neurotransmitter has more time in the synaptic cleft and a greater likelihood that the receiving neuron will receive the message. When you hear "SSRI" (the most common form of antidepressants), that stands for "Selective

Serotonin *Reuptake* Inhibitor". Our goal with these treatments is to increase cell signaling between neurons through this method.

You may wonder why we wouldn't just give patients more serotonin. This isn't currently possible because the serotonin molecule is too large to pass through the specialized layer that protects the brain from circulating blood (called the blood-brain barrier). Blood and its contents are toxic to the brain. Instead, nutrients are communicated to the brain through the blood-brain-barrier and into a specialized liquid called cerebrospinal fluid. It's normally clear like water. This design also protects us from getting brain infections. If bacteria or viruses that enter the bloodstream were able to pass seamlessly into the brain, many more people would get deadly brain infections. Serotonin, like bacteria and viruses, is too big to pass through the barrier, though it naturally occurs there. Instead, our SSRI medications are able to pass through. When it comes to increasing the quantity of serotonin, we look to improving diet and nutrition so that the body has the building blocks it needs to produce serotonin and other neurotransmitters as it is designed to do.

Pharmacological Treatment

For years, there have been two gold-standard treatments for OCD: Exposure and Response Prevention (ERP) and serotonergic medications. While these two remain the most effective and widely used treatments, emerging and alternative therapies, as well as neuromodulation techniques, have become popular options for those wishing to avoid medications or who have tried medications without relief.

Table 1 summarizes the most common medications used in OCD treatment. Though only some carry FDA approval, that does not mean that those without approval are ineffective or even less effective. Whether a pharmaceutical company decides to pursue FDA approval is as much a financial decision as a therapeutic decision. In both categories, you will see many medications commonly called "antidepressants". While these medications are frequently used in the treatment of depression, their particular serotonergic properties seem to make them effective in treating OCD. How serotonergic medications treat OCD specifically is not well understood; however, it is believed that key brain regions such as the CSTC loop may be inhibited by increased serotonin. Newer research does show that taking antidepressants results in structural changes in key brain regions associated with OCD.

FDA Approved Medications	Off-Label Medications
Prozac/fluoxetine	Lexapro/escitalopram
Zoloft/sertraline	Celexa/citalopram
Luvox/fluvoxamine	Risperdal/risperidone
Paxil/paroxetine	Abilify/aripiprazole
Anafranil/clomipramine	Lithobid/lithium
	Zofran/ondansetron

Tabe 1. Medications used in the treatment of OCD

Emerging and Alternative Treatments

Some of the same brain regions targeted by oral medications can be impacted through neuromodulation techniques (see Table 2). Neuromodulation has grown in popularity as our ability to target and apply a stimulus to specific brain regions has improved. Repetitive Transcranial Magnetic Stimulation (rTMS) uses electromagnets to send rapid and brief pulses into the brain. It is administered in a doctor's office, involves no invasive procedure, and generally produces no lasting side effects. The sensation feels something like a brief knocking on the scalp, but once patients get used to the feeling, some even fall asleep during treatment. It has existed for some time as a highly effective treatment for depression; its use in OCD is newer but promising.

Neurofeedback is another noninvasive potential treatment for OCD. Electrodes are placed on the scalp that read brain activity (note that nothing is being administered or applied to the brain). Brain activity is displayed visually on a computer monitor in front of the patient. Generally, a task (such as raising a ball or calming ripples in a pool) is displayed on the patient's computer monitor, and as their brain waves match the desired level, the corresponding task progresses on the screen. Through unconscious association, the brain learns to more consistently match the desired activity, thus producing a response even when patients are not connected to the device.

Deep Brain Stimulation and Electroconvulsive Therapy are reserved for the most resistant cases, though they represent a safe and effective option for patients requiring that level of care.

Neuromodulation Therapies
Repetitive Transcranial Magnetic Stimulation (rTMS)
Neurofeedback
Electroconvulsive Therapy (ECT)
Deep Brain Stimulation (DBS)

Table 2. Neuromodulation used in the treatment of OCD

Several other options exist for patients seeking to avoid daily prescribed medication (see Table 3), such as ketamine infusions and supplements. Ketamine is an anesthetic medication most commonly used in surgery since 1970. Its use in mental health conditions is more recent, though initial data is promising. Much lower doses than those used in anesthesia are infused via an IV over the course of about an hour. Patients may experience a slight dissociative experience (feeling separate from their body or that things around them seem off or less real), but this side effect quickly resolves once the infusion is complete. Several important neurotransmitters increase after ketamine infusions, and early research shows that regular counseling can increase their effectiveness.

Supplements that have shown promise in OCD are N-acetylcysteine (NAC) and Myo-inositol. They are generally very low in side effects and are relatively affordable. The difficulty with supplements is that they are not regulated by the FDA, so it's important to find a supplement company/brand that independent lab tests their products for purity and potency to assure you that what is in the capsule is what they state is in them on the front of the bottle. Other investigational supplements include curcumin, valerian root, zinc, vitamin B12, and folate. Remember to consult your medical provider before trying any supplements.

Alternative and Emerging Therapies
N-acetylcysteine (NAC)
Myo-inositol
Ketamine infusions
Under investigation: Curcumin, Valarian Root, Zinc, Vitamin B12 and Folate

Table 3. Alternative and Emerging therapies used in the treatment of OCD

Nonpharmacological Treatment

As we mentioned above, the gold standard nonpharmacologic treatment for OCD is ERP. Like its name suggests, it involves purposely exposing oneself to feared stimuli and preventing the corresponding compulsion (whether mental or behavioral). Repeated trials of this type of therapy work to put a wedge within the OCD cycle as illustrated in Figure 3.

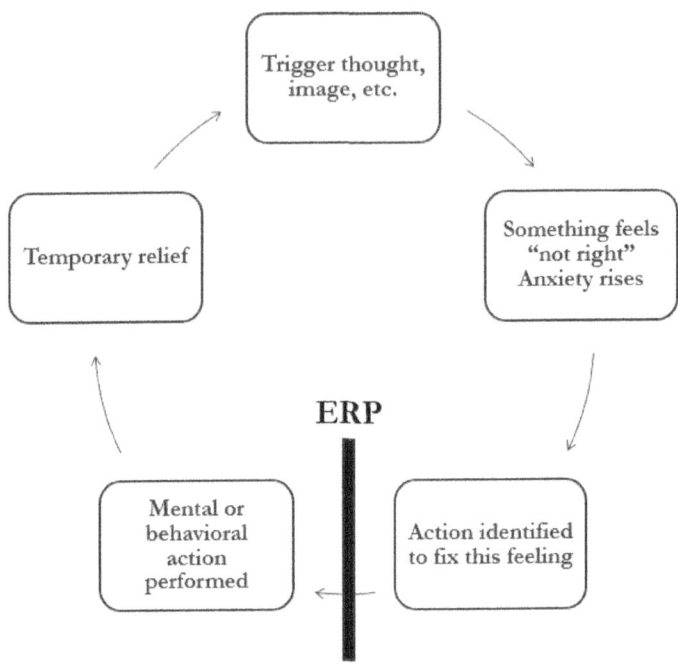

Figure 3. ERP mechanism within the Cognitive Behavioral Loop.

We often don't think about the compulsive behaviors or mental rituals as coping mechanisms, but that's exactly what they are. They are ways the brain has learned to reduce anxiety so that we remain functional temporarily. If the room I am currently sitting in caught fire, I would run out of the room. I'd feel a sigh of relief that I was safe and that behavior (of running out of the room) would become reinforced, so the next time something like that happened, I'm even more likely to run out of the room. The more we participate in the compulsive actions, the more reinforced they become, fueling the OCD loop.

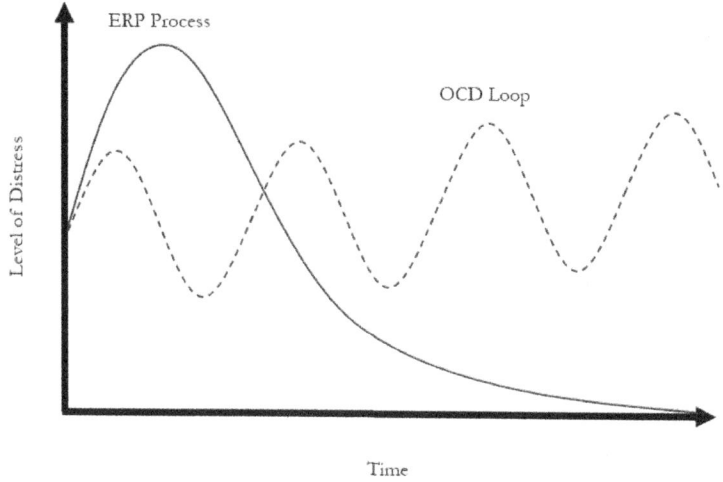

Figure 4. Comparing ERP Process to traditional OCD loop.

In Figure 4 above, the dotted line represents the OCD loop. A trigger occurs, and anxiety starts to rise. Our brains have realized that the most efficient way to reduce anxiety is to perform a corresponding compulsion or mental act (some may make sense to us such as washing our hands when we have intrusive thoughts of germs, others may not make as much sense to us like counting to a certain number to make sure something bad doesn't happen). Once a ritual has been performed, anxiety generally reduces slightly, but the problem is that the reduction doesn't last long. Shortly, anxiety rises again, and the cycle repeats.

ERP seeks to disrupt this process. The solid line in Figure 4 represents what happens when we use ERP to treat OCD. Because we prevent the compulsion that was previously helping keep anxiety at bay, our level of distress rises much higher (this is the hard part). Eventually, however, anxiety begins to decrease (that may take minutes or it could take hours), but it *will* eventually decrease. Anxiety *cannot* stay high forever. As it comes down, the brain realizes that we didn't need to do anything (meaning a compulsion) to get the anxiety to go away. A new association begins to be formed, and the old one involving compulsions begins to fade away. This doesn't happen after a single exposure, but with repeated exposures and preventing compulsions, anxiety drops well below the relief the old OCD loop used to produce.

The following sections will guide you through the steps to create and participate in an ERP program. Though a difficult process, the freedom produced on the other side of ERP is well worth the work.

Step 1

Obsessive and Compulsive Inventory

The first step in treating OCD is identifying certain thoughts and behaviors *as* OCD. Many times, OCD thoughts and rituals can become so much a part of someone's life that they no longer recognize them, or they go unnoticed. Though not comprehensive, the checklist below can be used to identify problematic obsessions and compulsions experienced by those with OCD. Check off any from the list that troubles you at least once a week or more. You may wish to denote using a different mark or color which obsessions or compulsions you are currently dealing with, as well as those you have dealt with in the past. This information will be used in the subsequent sections to craft an ERP regimen.

Obsessive Concerns Checklist

Aggressive Obsessions

- ☐ Actively hurting yourself or others
- ☐ Losing your mind and hurting someone else
- ☐ Gruesome images, thoughts, or words
- ☐ Accidentally saying an inappropriate/vulgar word or phrase
- ☐ Accidentally making an obscene gesture
- ☐ Hoping others will have an accident or become ill
- ☐ Other:

_____

Contamination Obsessions

- ☐ Bodily waste or fluids
- ☐ Dirt
- ☐ Germs/Viruses
- ☐ Chemicals
- ☐ Garbage
- ☐ Sticky or greasy items
- ☐ Concerns food or drink has been altered or tampered with
- ☐ Poisonous plants or animals
- ☐ Contact with living animals

- ☐ Contact with dead animals
- ☐ Contact with people
- ☐ Contact with people who look unclean or unkempt
- ☐ Contracting a disease or illness
- ☐ Spreading an illness
- ☐ Places where sickness is treated (hospitals or doctors' offices)
- ☐ Being contaminated by words or names of illness
- ☐ Personal items being impacted by being in the area when something unpleasant happened
- ☐ Other:

Harm, Danger, Loss, or Embarrassment Obsessions

- ☐ Having an accident
- ☐ Having an illness
- ☐ Causing harm to others through thoughts
- ☐ Causing harm to others through carelessness
- ☐ Never being able to be happy or get what you want in life
- ☐ Whether you harmed someone in the past
- ☐ Being taken advantage of by others
- ☐ Having taken advantage of someone else
- ☐ Insulting or offending others
- ☐ Damage to personal property
- ☐ Damage to others' property
- ☐ Acting inappropriately in public
- ☐ Being looked at or noticed by others critically
- ☐ Forgetting information such as facts, memories, appointments, etc.
- ☐ Your children not being your own
- ☐ Other:

Health and Body-Related Obsessions

- ☐ Parts of your body are ugly or disfigured
- ☐ Your body has scars or blemishes

☐ Wondering how certain parts of your body function
☐ A part of your body doesn't work properly
☐ Certain parts of your body are too large or small
☐ Concerns about your weight
☐ You will go bald or have thinning hair
☐ Clothing doesn't fit correctly
☐ You are aging prematurely
☐ You have brain damage or neurodegeneration
☐ You have an undiagnosed serious medical condition
☐ Other:

_____

Neutral Obsessions

☐ Repetitive questions for which there are no answers
☐ Awareness of certain things in your environment (sounds, colors, people, objects)
☐ Awareness of body functions (breathing, blinking, heart, etc)
☐ Awareness of abnormal body functions (aches/pains, stiffness, tinnitus)
☐ Other:

_____

Perfectionistic Obsessions

☐ Saying or doing things perfectly
☐ Having a perfect understanding of something
☐ Making sure others have perfectly understood what you said
☐ Wanting a perfect appearance or clothing to fit perfectly
☐ Keeping things perfectly ordered or clean
☐ Making things symmetrical
☐ Perfectly reading something and understanding it
☐ Perfectly communicating things through writing
☐ Other:

_____

Relational Obsessions

- ☐ You will be unfaithful to a partner
- ☐ Your partner might not be right for you
- ☐ You don't love your partner sufficiently
- ☐ That you will be trapped in an unsatisfactory relationship
- ☐ You may have offended or upset your partner in some way
- ☐ That your partner is mad or upset with you
- ☐ Other:

Religious Obsessions

Note: *Some of the following are only applicable to certain religions, others may not be listed that apply to your specific faith. Please use the "other" space to outline any that may be missed.*

- ☐ Being deliberately sinful or blasphemous
- ☐ Committing an unpardonable sin
- ☐ Not believing faith "sufficiently"
- ☐ Doubting certain aspects of faith (miracles, resurrection, etc.)
- ☐ Doubting that you are part of the faith
- ☐ Fear you may convert to another religion
- ☐ Fear of being possessed
- ☐ Fear you may have left something unconfessed
- ☐ That you haven't told the truth perfectly
- ☐ Needing to be perfectly religious
- ☐ Inappropriate thoughts about religious figures
- ☐ Blasphemous thoughts
- ☐ Taking communion in an unworthy manner
- ☐ That your baptism was false
- ☐ That you are not part of the "elect"
- ☐ Other:

Sexual Obsessions

- ☐ Forbidden/perverse thoughts or images
- ☐ Sex with children
- ☐ Sex with animals
- ☐ Incest
- ☐ Being homosexual or same-sex attracted
- ☐ Sex with religious figures
- ☐ Acting sexually toward others
- ☐ Wondering whether an action could be viewed sexually
- ☐ Wondering if you felt sexually aroused at inappropriate times or around the wrong people
- ☐ Other:

Superstitious or Magical Obsessions

- ☐ Having bad luck
- ☐ Lucky or unlucky numbers
- ☐ Lucky or unlucky colors, objections, or possessions
- ☐ That overheard bad events could cause those bad events in self or others
- ☐ Certain actions can cause bad luck
- ☐ Need to perform certain behaviors a certain number of times
- ☐ Lucky or unlucky thoughts
- ☐ Other:

Compulsive Activities Checklist

Body-Focused Compulsions

- ☐ Checking appearance in the mirror for problems
- ☐ Choosing what clothes to wear
- ☐ Questioning others about your appearance
- ☐ Having to have your appearance surgically altered or seeking medical advice about appearance
- ☐ Checking for symmetry or perfection in appearance

☐ Seeking medical consultations for possible illness
☐ Reading about illnesses online or in books
☐ Self-examination of body for signs of illness
☐ Having family check your body for signs of illness
☐ Discussing symptoms with family/friends
☐ Taking temperature
☐ Other:

Checking Compulsions

☐ Doors or windows for locks or that they are shut
☐ Water faucets
☐ Stoves
☐ Electrical appliances
☐ Lights
☐ Car doors/windows
☐ Mailboxes
☐ Extinguished cigarettes or matches
☐ Surfaces or objects for damage
☐ Your paperwork or writing for errors or obscenities
☐ Filling out forms
☐ Checking solved math
☐ Counting money
☐ That valuables were not thrown away accidently
☐ That you haven't left anything behind
☐ Other:

Counting Compulsions

☐ Counting while performing other behaviors (like walking, tapping pencil, etc.)
☐ Repeating behaviors a certain number of times
☐ Focusing on odd or even number of a particular behavior
☐ Doing something for a certain amount of time
☐ The number of objects in a specific area (on a table, bookshelf, etc.)

☐ Counting (unconnected to anything else)
☐ Other:

_____

Decontamination Compulsions

☐ Washing hands excessively or ritually
☐ Bathing/showering excessively or ritually
☐ Disinfecting yourself
☐ Disinfecting others
☐ Brushing teeth excessively
☐ Changing clothing frequently to avoid contamination
☐ Using gloves, paper, or cloth to touch things
☐ Performing certain thought rituals to remove contamination
☐ Questioning others about potential contamination
☐ Avoiding public objects or places (door handles, telephones, public transit, restrooms)
☐ Changing diapers
☐ Using toilet
☐ Visiting a hospital
☐ Handling money
☐ Handling food (especially raw/undercooked)
☐ Other:

_____

Magical/Undoing Compulsions

☐ Reciting or thinking certain words, names, sounds, etc.
☐ Moving body or gesturing in a specific way
☐ Mentally arranging certain thoughts in a specific way
☐ Stepping/walking in a certain way
☐ Performing actions or movements in reverse
☐ Washing off ideas or thoughts
☐ Rethinking thoughts
☐ Eating or not eating certain foods
☐ Looking at certain things or thinking certain things to cancel others out

☐ Touching things in a special way
☐ Other:

_____

Mental Compulsions

☐ Making mental maps of places
☐ Memorizing facts
☐ Making mental lists
☐ Learning everything about a particular subject
☐ Reviewing past situations to try to perfectly understand them
☐ Thinking particular thoughts in a specific way
☐ Creating mental images or pictures
☐ Repeating your own words or someone else's
☐ Rethinking thoughts
☐ Thinking thoughts in reverse
☐ Analyzing thoughts to determine if they were obsessions or not
☐ Other:

_____

Perfectionistic Compulsions

☐ Arrange objects in a special way
☐ Not using objects so they remain in perfect condition
☐ Buying only perfect items
☐ Keeping your home or living space perfectly clean/ordered
☐ Saying things perfectly
☐ Read or reread every work in a text to avoid missing things
☐ Remaking decisions to make sure you have made the perfect one
☐ Punishing yourself for not having behaved perfectly
☐ Telling the truth perfectly
☐ Performing activities until they feel just right
☐ Only performing some activities at exact times

☐ Other:

_____

Protective Compulsions

    ☐ Checking with others or your own memory to see if you have harmed or insulted someone
    ☐ Removing objects from environment that could cause harm
    ☐ Aversion to using sharp instruments
    ☐ Checking whereabouts of others to make sure they are okay
    ☐ Limiting others activities to avoid harm
    ☐ Warning others repeatedly of potential harm/danger
    ☐ Asking others if you will be safe
    ☐ Asking others if they will be safe
    ☐ Confessing things you believe may have caused harm to someone else
    ☐ Other:

_____

Relational Compulsions

    ☐ Apologizing
    ☐ Confessing/asking forgiveness for suspected offenses you may have committed against others
    ☐ Asking if relationship is "okay"
    ☐ Questioning whereabouts of significant other to make sure they are being faithful
    ☐ Observing who significant other looks at to make sure they are not being unfaithful
    ☐ Other:

_____

Touching or Movement Compulsions

    ☐ Gesturing or moving in a certain way
    ☐ Looking at something in a special way
    ☐ Movement in symmetrical or special ways
    ☐ Stepping in certain places while walking

- ☐ Head or neck movements in a special way
- ☐ Doing the opposite movement of what was just done
- ☐ Repeating movements until they "feel right"
- ☐ Touching surfaces, edges, or parts of things
- ☐ Other:

_____

Grooming Impulsions

- ☐ Hair pulling
- ☐ Skin picking or biting
- ☐ Nail biting or picking
- ☐ Picking or squeezing pimples or blemishes (above cosmetic treatment)
- ☐ Other:

_____

Hoarding/Collecting Compulsions/Impulsions

- ☐ Saving broken or useless items
- ☐ Buying multiples of items beyond what is reasonable
- ☐ Searching through your own or others trash
- ☐ Struggling to throw things away
- ☐ Saving informational matter (newspaper, magazines, junk mail)
- ☐ Keeping lists or records of items
- ☐ Other:

_____

Self-Mutilating Impulsions

- ☐ Cutting or scratching yourself
- ☐ Burning yourself
- ☐ Poking yourself in the eye
- ☐ Biting yourself
- ☐ Other:

_____

Once the obsessions and compulsions that are present have been identified, it is important to begin understanding the relationship between the intrusive obsessive thought and its corresponding compulsion(s). The following table can be used to note the relationship between particular obsessions and compulsions.

Obsession	Compulsion
Example: *Fear of Contamination*	Example: *Washing Hands*

OCD Treatment Journal

Step 2

Subjective Units of Distress Scale

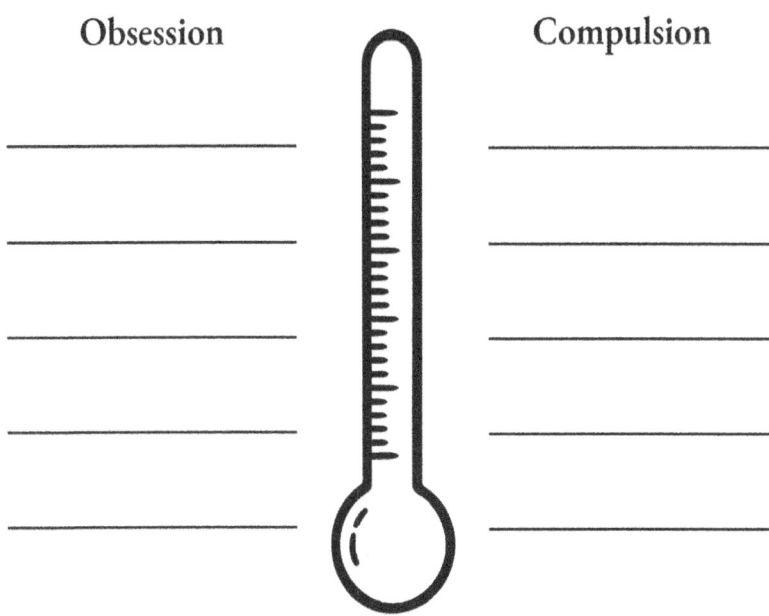

Figure 5. The Subjective Units of Distress Scale (SUDS) thermometer.

Next, we need to grade particular obsessions and compulsions by the level of distress they cause. Some obsession/compulsion loops may cause only mild distress, while others may be more severe. Unlike other measuring tools we use in medicine, distress (much like physical pain) doesn't have an objective measurement device. In OCD research and treatment, the Subjective Units of Distress Scale (SUDS) is often used to display how much distress a particular intrusive thought or compulsion causes a patient. Think of the level of distress like the fluid in a thermometer, as shown in Figure 5. Lower levels of distress would be represented by fluid toward the bottom of the thermometer, while higher levels of distress would raise the fluid all the way to the top. The SUDS can be completed using either a 0-10 or 0-100 scale, whichever you prefer. Spend some time assigning each obsession and compulsion a SUDS score. They will then be ranked in the next section.

Step 3

Obsessive and Compulsive Ranking

Although it is usually the most distressing obsessions and compulsions that cause us the most impact in our day-to-day life, ERP is best completed by starting not with the most distressing but the less distressing loops first. There are several reasons for this. Starting with the most distressing loops can cause an exacerbation (worsening) of both those loops and those below. Think of it like going to the gym, if you walked in to grab the heaviest weight first, you could strain your muscles and cause harm. If, however, you start with a lower weight and work your way up, by the time you reach the heaviest weight, it will feel much lighter than if you had started there. Another reason to start toward the lower end is that it gives us time to practice the exposure technique. Like training wheels on a bike, we want to gain some experience before taking on bigger challenges.

Use this space to rank each obsession/compulsion from most distressing to least distressing.

Obsession/Compulsion	SUDS (0-100 or 0-10)
	Most Distressing
	Least Distressing

Step 4

Exposures

Next, we begin the actual exposures. Exposures should be crafted such that they create a moderate level of anxiety but not panic attacks, around 6-8/10 (or 60-80/100) on the SUDS. If you have difficulty getting distress to that level try focusing on the elements of uncertainty present in any particular intrusive thought. Try to keep that distressing image, situation, impulse in your consciousness. Unlike other treatments in psychiatry, we don't want to use various coping skills like distraction while performing ERP. Instead we try to keep that anxiety elevated.

An example of an exposure may be putting one's hand near a trashcan if there is a fear of contamination. We prevent both removal of the hand from that environment as well as the usual compulsion (hand washing, showering, etc.). Anxiety will rise dramatically, well above where it would have should the compulsions have been performed but trust the process. By not using compulsions to keep anxiety at bay we break the cycle.

For those struggling with scrupulosity OCD, it may be reading particular passages of scripture that talk about the punishment of evil or the guilt present in all humankind. Or it could be reading particular passages that instill doubt (perhaps reading the miracles of Jesus, his resurrection, or second coming in Revelation). Keep that sense of uncertainty and lack of control at the front of your mind. As a fellow believer, it seems wrong to tell someone not to pray or read more scripture to comfort oneself, but that instruction is exactly what will produce the freedom to read or pray, not out of compulsion, but out of a peaceful desire to know God more.

How do we know an exposure is complete? Generally, when the distress falls below a 3/10 (30/100), it serves as a good indicator. With my patients, I've often said that if your compulsion is washing your hands because of intrusive thoughts of germs, you are free to wash your hands at the moment when you think, "I could wash my hands, but I don't have to". That's the result of ERP: being able to do normal things, such as washing hands, praying, and counting, not out of compulsion, but in freedom. If you feel you are being taken hostage (ie. "do this or else"), the

OCD loop remains in place. Through ERP, you will feel that internal demand decreases and freedom takes its place.

ERP is hard work. Don't grow discouraged. You know you're doing it correctly if it's difficult. Not many patients are asked to confront their worst fears on a daily or weekly basis; it takes incredible strength to undertake the work you are doing.

The logs that follow are a place to record your formal ERP exercise. They have a space to put the trigger situation or thought, the corresponding compulsion we are preventing, as well as a place to document distress over time using the SUD scale. While certain time increments are listed, some distress may take much longer to resolve; feel free to use whatever intervals you would like.

Date	Exposure The anxiety-provoking situation.	Compulsion Prevented The behavior or mental ritual we are preventing.	SUDS Scale			
			5min	10min	15min	20min
	Example: *Touching dirty dishes*	Example: *Handwashing*	7	7	5	2
			☐	☐	☐	☐
			☐	☐	☐	☐
			☐	☐	☐	☐
			☐	☐	☐	☐
			☐	☐	☐	☐
			☐	☐	☐	☐

Date	Exposure The anxiety-provoking situation.	Compulsion Prevented The behavior or mental ritual we are preventing.	SUDS Scale 5min 10min 15min 20min
			☐ ☐ ☐ ☐
			☐ ☐ ☐ ☐
			☐ ☐ ☐ ☐
			☐ ☐ ☐ ☐
			☐ ☐ ☐ ☐
			☐ ☐ ☐ ☐
			☐ ☐ ☐ ☐
			☐ ☐ ☐ ☐

Date	Exposure The anxiety-provoking situation.	Compulsion Prevented The behavior or mental ritual we are preventing.	SUDS Scale 5min 10min 15min 20min
			☐ ☐ ☐ ☐
			☐ ☐ ☐ ☐
			☐ ☐ ☐ ☐
			☐ ☐ ☐ ☐
			☐ ☐ ☐ ☐
			☐ ☐ ☐ ☐
			☐ ☐ ☐ ☐
			☐ ☐ ☐ ☐

Date	Exposure The anxiety-provoking situation.	Compulsion Prevented The behavior or mental ritual we are preventing.	SUDS Scale 5min 10min 15min 20min
			☐ ☐ ☐ ☐
			☐ ☐ ☐ ☐
			☐ ☐ ☐ ☐
			☐ ☐ ☐ ☐

Date	Exposure The anxiety-provoking situation.	Compulsion Prevented The behavior or mental ritual we are preventing.	SUDS Scale 5min 10min 15min 20min
			☐ ☐ ☐ ☐
			☐ ☐ ☐ ☐
			☐ ☐ ☐ ☐
			☐ ☐ ☐ ☐
			☐ ☐ ☐ ☐
			☐ ☐ ☐ ☐
			☐ ☐ ☐ ☐
			☐ ☐ ☐ ☐

OCD Treatment Journal

Date	Exposure The anxiety-provoking situation.	Compulsion Prevented The behavior or mental ritual we are preventing.	SUDS Scale 5min 10min 15min 20min
			☐ ☐ ☐ ☐
			☐ ☐ ☐ ☐
			☐ ☐ ☐ ☐
			☐ ☐ ☐ ☐
			☐ ☐ ☐ ☐
			☐ ☐ ☐ ☐
			☐ ☐ ☐ ☐
			☐ ☐ ☐ ☐

Date	Exposure The anxiety-provoking situation.	Compulsion Prevented The behavior or mental ritual we are preventing.	SUDS Scale			
			5min	10min	15min	20min
			☐	☐	☐	☐
			☐	☐	☐	☐
			☐	☐	☐	☐
			☐	☐	☐	☐
			☐	☐	☐	☐
			☐	☐	☐	☐
			☐	☐	☐	☐
			☐	☐	☐	☐

Date	Exposure The anxiety-provoking situation.	Compulsion Prevented The behavior or mental ritual we are preventing.	SUDS Scale 5min 10min 15min 20min
			☐ ☐ ☐ ☐
			☐ ☐ ☐ ☐
			☐ ☐ ☐ ☐
			☐ ☐ ☐ ☐
			☐ ☐ ☐ ☐
			☐ ☐ ☐ ☐
			☐ ☐ ☐ ☐
			☐ ☐ ☐ ☐

Date	Exposure The anxiety-provoking situation.	Compulsion Prevented The behavior or mental ritual we are preventing.	SUDS Scale			
			5min	10min	15min	20min
			☐	☐	☐	☐
			☐	☐	☐	☐
			☐	☐	☐	☐
			☐	☐	☐	☐
			☐	☐	☐	☐
			☐	☐	☐	☐
			☐	☐	☐	☐
			☐	☐	☐	☐

Date	Exposure The anxiety-provoking situation.	Compulsion Prevented The behavior or mental ritual we are preventing.	SUDS Scale 5min 10min 15min 20min
			☐ ☐ ☐ ☐
			☐ ☐ ☐ ☐
			☐ ☐ ☐ ☐
			☐ ☐ ☐ ☐
			☐ ☐ ☐ ☐
			☐ ☐ ☐ ☐
			☐ ☐ ☐ ☐
			☐ ☐ ☐ ☐

Step 5

Tracking

The most commonly used objective measure in research and practice is the Yale-Brown Obsessive-Compulsive Scale (Y-BOCS). This form screens for the prevalence and severity of both obsessions and compulsions. Several are included in this journal.

Watching the Y-BOCS score decrease is a rewarding process. Of course, it is important to remember that this is just a number and what matters most is how you are feeling, subjectively, but seeing progress on an objective measure can encourage you as you walk through ERP. Below is a space to record Y-BOCS scores you complete throughout the process. I would recommend completing a Y-BOCS around once every 2 weeks to 1 month throughout ERP.

Date	YBOCS Score

Yale-Brown Obsessive Compulsive Scale (Y-BOCS)

8-15 = Mild OCD; 16-23 = Moderate OCD; 24-31 = Severe OCD; 32-40 = Extreme OCD

Obsessions are frequent, unwelcome, and intrusive thoughts.	0	1	2	3	4
1. How much time do you spend on obsessive thoughts?	None	0-1 hrs/day	1-3 hrs/day	3-8 hrs/day	More than 8 hrs/day
2. How much do your obsessive thoughts interfere with your personal, social, or work life?	None	Mild	Definite but manageable	Substantial interference	Severe
3. How much do your obsessive thoughts distress you?	None	Little	Moderate but manageable	Severe	Nearly constant, disabling
4. How hard do you try to resist your obsessions?	Always try	Try much of the time	Try some of the time	Rarely try, often yield.	Never try, completely yield
5. How much control do you have over your obsessive thoughts?	Complete control	Much control	Some control	Little Control	No control

Compulsions are repetitive behaviors or mental acts that you have a strong urge to repeat that are aimed at reducing your anxiety or preventing some dreaded event.	0	1	2	3	4
6. How much time do you spend performing compulsive behaviors?	None	0-1 hrs/day	1-3 hrs/day	3-8 hrs/day	More than 8 hrs/day
7. How much do your compulsive behaviors interfere with your personal, social, or work life?	None	Mild	Definite but manageable	Substantial interference	Severe
8. How anxious would you feel if you were prevented from performing your compulsive behaviors?	None	Little	Moderate but manageable	Severe	Nearly constant, disabling
9. How hard do you try to resist your compulsive behaviors?	Always try	Try much of the time	Try some of the time	Rarely try, often yield.	Never try, completely yield
10. How much control do you have over your compulsive behaviors?	Complete control	Much control	Some control	Little Control	No control

Total: _____

Yale-Brown Obsessive Compulsive Scale (Y-BOCS)

8-15 = Mild OCD; 16-23 = Moderate OCD; 24-31 = Severe OCD; 32-40 = Extreme OCD

Obsessions are frequent, unwelcome, and intrusive thoughts.	0	1	2	3	4
1. How much time do you spend on obsessive thoughts?	None	0-1 hrs/day	1-3 hrs/day	3-8 hrs/day	More than 8 hrs/day
2. How much do your obsessive thoughts interfere with your personal, social, or work life?	None	Mild	Definite but manageable	Substantial interference	Severe
3. How much do your obsessive thoughts distress you?	None	Little	Moderate but manageable	Severe	Nearly constant, disabling
4. How hard do you try to resist your obsessions?	Always try	Try much of the time	Try some of the time	Rarely try, often yield.	Never try, completely yield
5. How much control do you have over your obsessive thoughts?	Complete control	Much control	Some control	Little Control	No control

Compulsions are repetitive behaviors or mental acts that you have a strong urge to repeat that are aimed at reducing your anxiety or preventing some dreaded event.	0	1	2	3	4
6. How much time do you spend performing compulsive behaviors?	None	0-1 hrs/day	1-3 hrs/day	3-8 hrs/day	More than 8 hrs/day
7. How much do your compulsive behaviors interfere with your personal, social, or work life?	None	Mild	Definite but manageable	Substantial interference	Severe
8. How anxious would you feel if you were prevented from performing your compulsive behaviors?	None	Little	Moderate but manageable	Severe	Nearly constant, disabling
9. How hard do you try to resist your compulsive behaviors?	Always try	Try much of the time	Try some of the time	Rarely try, often yield.	Never try, completely yield
10. How much control do you have over your compulsive behaviors?	Complete control	Much control	Some control	Little Control	No control

Total: _____

59

Yale-Brown Obsessive Compulsive Scale (Y-BOCS)

8-15 = Mild OCD; 16-23 = Moderate OCD; 24-31 = Severe OCD; 32-40 = Extreme OCD

Obsessions are frequent, unwelcome, and intrusive thoughts.	0	1	2	3	4
1. How much time do you spend on obsessive thoughts?	None	0-1 hrs/day	1-3 hrs/day	3-8 hrs/day	More than 8 hrs/day
2. How much do your obsessive thoughts interfere with your personal, social, or work life?	None	Mild	Definite but manageable	Substantial interference	Severe
3. How much do your obsessive thoughts distress you?	None	Little	Moderate but manageable	Severe	Nearly constant, disabling
4. How hard do you try to resist your obsessions?	Always try	Try much of the time	Try some of the time	Rarely try, often yield.	Never try, completely yield
5. How much control do you have over your obsessive thoughts?	Complete control	Much control	Some control	Little Control	No control

Compulsions are repetitive behaviors or mental acts that you have a strong urge to repeat that are aimed at reducing your anxiety or preventing some dreaded event.	0	1	2	3	4
6. How much time do you spend performing compulsive behaviors?	None	0-1 hrs/day	1-3 hrs/day	3-8 hrs/day	More than 8 hrs/ day
7. How much do your compulsive behaviors interfere with your personal, social, or work life?	None	Mild	Definite but manageable	Substantial interference	Severe
8. How anxious would you feel if you were prevented from performing your compulsive behaviors?	None	Little	Moderate but manageable	Severe	Nearly constant, disabling
9. How hard do you try to resist your compulsive behaviors?	Always try	Try much of the time	Try some of the time	Rarely try, often yield.	Never try, completely yield
10. How much control do you have over your compulsive behaviors?	Complete control	Much control	Some control	Little Control	No control

Total: _____

Yale–Brown Obsessive Compulsive Scale (Y-BOCS)

8-15 = Mild OCD; 16-23 = Moderate OCD; 24-31 = Severe OCD; 32-40 = Extreme OCD

Obsessions are frequent, unwelcome, and intrusive thoughts.	0	1	2	3	4
1. How much time do you spend on obsessive thoughts?	None	0-1 hrs/day	1-3 hrs/day	3-8 hrs/day	More than 8 hrs/day
2. How much do your obsessive thoughts interfere with your personal, social, or work life?	None	Mild	Definite but manageable	Substantial interference	Severe
3. How much do your obsessive thoughts distress you?	None	Little	Moderate but manageable	Severe	Nearly constant, disabling
4. How hard do you try to resist your obsessions?	Always try	Try much of the time	Try some of the time	Rarely try, often yield.	Never try, completely yield
5. How much control do you have over your obsessive thoughts?	Complete control	Much control	Some control	Little Control	No control

Compulsions are repetitive behaviors or mental acts that you have a strong urge to repeat that are aimed at reducing your anxiety or preventing some dreaded event.	0	1	2	3	4
6. How much time do you spend performing compulsive behaviors?	None	0-1 hrs/day	1-3 hrs/day	3-8 hrs/day	More than 8 hrs/day
7. How much do your compulsive behaviors interfere with your personal, social, or work life?	None	Mild	Definite but manageable	Substantial interference	Severe
8. How anxious would you feel if you were prevented from performing your compulsive behaviors?	None	Little	Moderate but manageable	Severe	Nearly constant, disabling
9. How hard do you try to resist your compulsive behaviors?	Always try	Try much of the time	Try some of the time	Rarely try, often yield.	Never try, completely yield
10. How much control do you have over your compulsive behaviors?	Complete control	Much control	Some control	Little Control	No control

Total: _____

Yale-Brown Obsessive Compulsive Scale (Y-BOCS)

8-15 = Mild OCD; 16-23 = Moderate OCD; 24-31 = Severe OCD; 32-40 = Extreme OCD

Obsessions are frequent, unwelcome, and intrusive thoughts.	0	1	2	3	4
1. How much time do you spend on obsessive thoughts?	None	0-1 hrs/day	1-3 hrs/day	3-8 hrs/day	More than 8 hrs/ day
2. How much do your obsessive thoughts interfere with your personal, social, or work life?	None	Mild	Definite but manageable	Substantial interference	Severe
3. How much do your obsessive thoughts distress you?	None	Little	Moderate but manageable	Severe	Nearly constant, disabling
4. How hard do you try to resist your obsessions?	Always try	Try much of the time	Try some of the time	Rarely try, often yield.	Never try, completely yield
5. How much control do you have over your obsessive thoughts?	Complete control	Much control	Some control	Little Control	No control

Compulsions are repetitive behaviors or mental acts that you have a strong urge to repeat that are aimed at reducing your anxiety or preventing some dreaded event.	0	1	2	3	4
6. How much time do you spend performing compulsive behaviors?	None	0-1 hrs/day	1-3 hrs/day	3-8 hrs/day	More than 8 hrs/day
7. How much do your compulsive behaviors interfere with your personal, social, or work life?	None	Mild	Definite but manageable	Substantial interference	Severe
8. How anxious would you feel if you were prevented from performing your compulsive behaviors?	None	Little	Moderate but manageable	Severe	Nearly constant, disabling
9. How hard do you try to resist your compulsive behaviors?	Always try	Try much of the time	Try some of the time	Rarely try, often yield.	Never try, completely yield
10. How much control do you have over your compulsive behaviors?	Complete control	Much control	Some control	Little Control	No control

Total: _____

Yale-Brown Obsessive Compulsive Scale (Y-BOCS)

8-15 = Mild OCD; 16-23 = Moderate OCD; 24-31 = Severe OCD; 32-40 = Extreme OCD

Obsessions are frequent, unwelcome, and intrusive thoughts.	0	1	2	3	4
1. How much time do you spend on obsessive thoughts?	None	0-1 hrs/day	1-3 hrs/day	3-8 hrs/day	More than 8 hrs/ day
2. How much do your obsessive thoughts interfere with your personal, social, or work life?	None	Mild	Definite but manageable	Substantial interference	Severe
3. How much do your obsessive thoughts distress you?	None	Little	Moderate but manageable	Severe	Nearly constant, disabling
4. How hard do you try to resist your obsessions?	Always try	Try much of the time	Try some of the time	Rarely try, often yield.	Never try, completely yield
5. How much control do you have over your obsessive thoughts?	Complete control	Much control	Some control	Little Control	No control

Compulsions are repetitive behaviors or mental acts that you have a strong urge to repeat that are aimed at reducing your anxiety or preventing some dreaded event.	0	1	2	3	4
6. How much time do you spend performing compulsive behaviors?	None	0-1 hrs/day	1-3 hrs/day	3-8 hrs/day	More than 8 hrs/day
7. How much do your compulsive behaviors interfere with your personal, social, or work life?	None	Mild	Definite but manageable	Substantial interference	Severe
8. How anxious would you feel if you were prevented from performing your compulsive behaviors?	None	Little	Moderate but manageable	Severe	Nearly constant, disabling
9. How hard do you try to resist your compulsive behaviors?	Always try	Try much of the time	Try some of the time	Rarely try, often yield.	Never try, completely yield
10. How much control do you have over your compulsive behaviors?	Complete control	Much control	Some control	Little Control	No control

Total: _____

Yale-Brown Obsessive Compulsive Scale (Y-BOCS)

8-15 = Mild OCD; 16-23 = Moderate OCD; 24-31 = Severe OCD; 32-40 = Extreme OCD

Obsessions are frequent, unwelcome, and intrusive thoughts.	0	1	2	3	4
1. How much time do you spend on obsessive thoughts?	None	0-1 hrs/day	1-3 hrs/day	3-8 hrs/day	More than 8 hrs/day
2. How much do your obsessive thoughts interfere with your personal, social, or work life?	None	Mild	Definite but manageable	Substantial interference	Severe
3. How much do your obsessive thoughts distress you?	None	Little	Moderate but manageable	Severe	Nearly constant, disabling
4. How hard do you try to resist your obsessions?	Always try	Try much of the time	Try some of the time	Rarely try, often yield.	Never try, completely yield
5. How much control do you have over your obsessive thoughts?	Complete control	Much control	Some control	Little Control	No control

Compulsions are repetitive behaviors or mental acts that you have a strong urge to repeat that are aimed at reducing your anxiety or preventing some dreaded event.	0	1	2	3	4
6. How much time do you spend performing compulsive behaviors?	None	0-1 hrs/day	1-3 hrs/day	3-8 hrs/day	More than 8 hrs/day
7. How much do your compulsive behaviors interfere with your personal, social, or work life?	None	Mild	Definite but manageable	Substantial interference	Severe
8. How anxious would you feel if you were prevented from performing your compulsive behaviors?	None	Little	Moderate but manageable	Severe	Nearly constant, disabling
9. How hard do you try to resist your compulsive behaviors?	Always try	Try much of the time	Try some of the time	Rarely try, often yield.	Never try, completely yield
10. How much control do you have over your compulsive behaviors?	Complete control	Much control	Some control	Little Control	No control

Total: _____

Yale-Brown Obsessive Compulsive Scale (Y-BOCS)

8-15 = Mild OCD; 16-23 = Moderate OCD; 24-31 = Severe OCD; 32-40 = Extreme OCD

Obsessions are frequent, unwelcome, and intrusive thoughts.	0	1	2	3	4
1. How much time do you spend on obsessive thoughts?	None	0-1 hrs/day	1-3 hrs/day	3-8 hrs/day	More than 8 hrs/day
2. How much do your obsessive thoughts interfere with your personal, social, or work life?	None	Mild	Definite but manageable	Substantial interference	Severe
3. How much do your obsessive thoughts distress you?	None	Little	Moderate but manageable	Severe	Nearly constant, disabling
4. How hard do you try to resist your obsessions?	Always try	Try much of the time	Try some of the time	Rarely try, often yield.	Never try, completely yield
5. How much control do you have over your obsessive thoughts?	Complete control	Much control	Some control	Little Control	No control

Compulsions are repetitive behaviors or mental acts that you have a strong urge to repeat that are aimed at reducing your anxiety or preventing some dreaded event.	0	1	2	3	4
6. How much time do you spend performing compulsive behaviors?	None	0-1 hrs/day	1-3 hrs/day	3-8 hrs/day	More than 8 hrs/day
7. How much do your compulsive behaviors interfere with your personal, social, or work life?	None	Mild	Definite but manageable	Substantial interference	Severe
8. How anxious would you feel if you were prevented from performing your compulsive behaviors?	None	Little	Moderate but manageable	Severe	Nearly constant, disabling
9. How hard do you try to resist your compulsive behaviors?	Always try	Try much of the time	Try some of the time	Rarely try, often yield.	Never try, completely yield
10. How much control do you have over your compulsive behaviors?	Complete control	Much control	Some control	Little Control	No control

Total: _____

71

Yale-Brown Obsessive Compulsive Scale (Y-BOCS)

8-15 = Mild OCD; 16-23 = Moderate OCD; 24-31 = Severe OCD; 32-40 = Extreme OCD

Obsessions are frequent, unwelcome, and intrusive thoughts.	0	1	2	3	4
1. How much time do you spend on obsessive thoughts?	None	0-1 hrs/day	1-3 hrs/day	3-8 hrs/day	More than 8 hrs/day
2. How much do your obsessive thoughts interfere with your personal, social, or work life?	None	Mild	Definite but manageable	Substantial interference	Severe
3. How much do your obsessive thoughts distress you?	None	Little	Moderate but manageable	Severe	Nearly constant, disabling
4. How hard do you try to resist your obsessions?	Always try	Try much of the time	Try some of the time	Rarely try, often yield.	Never try, completely yield
5. How much control do you have over your obsessive thoughts?	Complete control	Much control	Some control	Little Control	No control

Compulsions are repetitive behaviors or mental acts that you have a strong urge to repeat that are aimed at reducing your anxiety or preventing some dreaded event.	0	1	2	3	4
6. How much time do you spend performing compulsive behaviors?	None	0-1 hrs/day	1-3 hrs/day	3-8 hrs/day	More than 8 hrs/ day
7. How much do your compulsive behaviors interfere with your personal, social, or work life?	None	Mild	Definite but manageable	Substantial interference	Severe
8. How anxious would you feel if you were prevented from performing your compulsive behaviors?	None	Little	Moderate but manageable	Severe	Nearly constant, disabling
9. How hard do you try to resist your compulsive behaviors?	Always try	Try much of the time	Try some of the time	Rarely try, often yield.	Never try, completely yield
10. How much control do you have over your compulsive behaviors?	Complete control	Much control	Some control	Little Control	No control

Total: _____

Yale-Brown Obsessive Compulsive Scale (Y-BOCS)

8-15 = Mild OCD; 16-23 = Moderate OCD; 24-31 = Severe OCD; 32-40 = Extreme OCD

Obsessions are frequent, unwelcome, and intrusive thoughts.	0	1	2	3	4
1. How much time do you spend on obsessive thoughts?	None	0-1 hrs/day	1-3 hrs/day	3-8 hrs/day	More than 8 hrs/day
2. How much do your obsessive thoughts interfere with your personal, social, or work life?	None	Mild	Definite but manageable	Substantial interference	Severe
3. How much do your obsessive thoughts distress you?	None	Little	Moderate but manageable	Severe	Nearly constant, disabling
4. How hard do you try to resist your obsessions?	Always try	Try much of the time	Try some of the time	Rarely try, often yield.	Never try, completely yield
5. How much control do you have over your obsessive thoughts?	Complete control	Much control	Some control	Little Control	No control

Compulsions are repetitive behaviors or mental acts that you have a strong urge to repeat that are aimed at reducing your anxiety or preventing some dreaded event.	0	1	2	3	4
6. How much time do you spend performing compulsive behaviors?	None	0-1 hrs/day	1-3 hrs/day	3-8 hrs/day	More than 8 hrs/day
7. How much do your compulsive behaviors interfere with your personal, social, or work life?	None	Mild	Definite but manageable	Substantial interference	Severe
8. How anxious would you feel if you were prevented from performing your compulsive behaviors?	None	Little	Moderate but manageable	Severe	Nearly constant, disabling
9. How hard do you try to resist your compulsive behaviors?	Always try	Try much of the time	Try some of the time	Rarely try, often yield.	Never try, completely yield
10. How much control do you have over your compulsive behaviors?	Complete control	Much control	Some control	Little Control	No control

Total: _____

Final Notes

As I mentioned before, it takes great strength to confront one's greatest fears. The difficulties you now face are producing for you something good, as Elisabeth Elliot said, "Suffering is never for nothing." OCD often comes and goes; there may be times of remission with little to no intrusive thoughts or compulsions (those times are lengthened and more frequent because of the hard work of ERP), other times may feel like a daily or hourly battle, but don't lose heart! Remember that the measure of suffering allotted to you is not infinite; it has been set and has a limit. One day, you will not suffer with OCD any longer, and though it may seem impossible now, we can affirm that one day we will say of this side of heaven, "I see why He did it this way."

Until that day comes. Beside you in the battle,

Appendix 1 – Note about OCD Traits

We've all heard people say, off-handedly, "I'm so OCD". What they are often referring to are certain peculiarities in the way they like things or the need to do something a certain way. They may also point to parents or grandparents who had a diagnosis of OCD and describe how they experience similar symptoms to them, but not to the same degree. Many, many people will experience an occasional symptom that shares similarities to those who have diagnosable OCD, but that doesn't mean everyone who has these symptoms also has OCD. The graph below in Figure 6 is meant to represent what a distribution of OCD symptoms might look like in the general population, while the bold line represents the cutoff for making a diagnosis of OCD. The difference between the occasional symptom and OCD has to do with a patient's level of functionality. The *DSM* requires there to be functional impairment as a result of the symptoms to make the diagnosis of OCD.

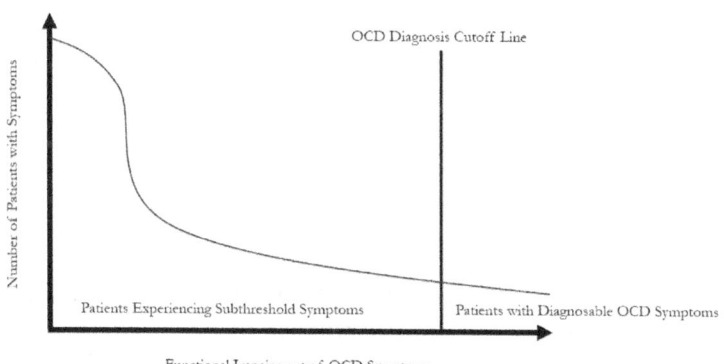

Figure 6. Prevalence of OCD symptoms and diagnosis.

In my medical training, professors told a story of a man who, each morning, would take on and take off each of his articles of clothing four times before leaving, or else he felt something bad might happen. When asking him about his symptoms, he didn't seem bothered by the need to perform this ritual; he wasn't missing any deadlines at work or neglecting anything at home. Without either the distress or functional impairment present, he didn't technically meet criteria for a diagnosis of OCD. It's important that psychiatry doesn't pathologize the small differences that make us unique and life interesting. It isn't the role of psychiatry to make everyone the same; it's to help those who are experiencing distress or functional impairment due to cognitive or behavioral symptoms. So the person experiencing the occasional symptom may feel "so OCD" about certain things, but until it impacts their life or causes significant distress, it's just one of those personality quirks.

Appendix 2 – Note about Scrupulosity

One of the most distressing things about OCD is that it seems to attack the things we care about most. It may be family, friends, career, our health, or it could be our relationship with God. Scrupulosity is especially distressing for believers because faith exists at the core of who we are. Additionally, many patients with scrupulosity OCD will lament that with other forms of OCD there's a sense of finality to some of the worries (eg. I fear contracting an illness and within a few days without illness I have proof nothing happened). With scrupulosity OCD, they will ask, "How can it be proven that they are of the elect, forgiven, in right standing with God, except in death?" The desire to resolve uncertainty and for control over things for which we have no control is especially prevalent in scrupulosity OCD.

It is a great act of faith to fall completely into God's sovereignty such that we realize we can do nothing to save ourselves; it is entirely, from start to finish, a work of the Holy Spirit. We must relinquish our desire to control and allow God to take that place. He speaks to us as he did to Job: "Where were you when I laid the foundations of the earth? Tell me, if you have understanding" (38:4).

All of the power and strength required to save you and keep you, forgive you, and bring you back when you wander, comes from your savior, as it was said of Jesus, "This was to fulfill the word that he had spoken: 'Of those whom you gave me I have lost not one'" (John 18:9).

When OCD attacks what you care about most and says you must do something to protect those things, may we all have the strength to deliver that care into the arms of the only one with the power to actually protect and rest as the Psalm instructs, "O LORD, my heart is not lifted up; my eyes are not raised too high; I do not occupy myself with things too great and too marvelous for me. But I have calmed and quieted my soul, like a weaned child with its mother; like a weaned child is my soul within me" (131:1-2).

Appendix 3 – OCD and the Reformation - Luther and Bunyan

Though devils all the world should fill,
All eager to devour us,
We tremble not, we fear no ill;
They shall not overpow'r us.
This world's prince may still
Scowl fierce as he will,
He can harm us none.
He's judged; the deed is done;
One little word can fell him.

-Martin Luther "A mighty Fortress is our God, A trusty Shield and Weapon"

The man who penned the words to the hymn above and would stand before the Diet of Worms and say boldly, "Unless I am convinced by Scripture and plain reason... I cannot and I will not recant anything for to go against conscience is neither right nor safe. God help me. Amen," was the same man who struggled intensely with doubts about his salvation as well as recurrent violent, lustful, and blasphemous intrusive images. God, in his sovereignty, ordained that Luther's hardship would also be the road through which he would reform His church and bring Luther into a closer relationship with Him.

Though the standards of diagnosis were not present during Luther's time, exploration into his writings and biographical data has long suggested that Luther struggled with what a modern psychologist or psychiatrist would define as OCD.

While OCD asks us to *do* something about the distress that we feel, freedom is found in surrendering to our ultimate powerlessness and trusting in the unchallenged sovereignty of the one who is in control. Luther's first attempts to address the intrusive thoughts of damnation, blasphemy, and lust were through his belief in the practices of the Catholic Church.

He writes:

"When I was a monk, I used to think that my salvation was undone... Therefore, I could not find peace, but I was constantly crucified by thoughts as these: 'You have committed this or that sin; you are guilty of envy, impatience, etc.'"

Later, he says:

"My conscience could never achieve certainty but was always in doubt and said: 'You have not done this correctly. You were not contrite enough. You omitted this in your confession... I was nursing incessant mistrust, doubt, fear, hatred and blasphemy against God. I was superstitious to the point of delirium and insanity."

His confessors grew restless as he used to present for confession for up to six hours at a time, "Look here, if you expect Christ to forgive you, come in with something to forgive—parricide, blasphemy, adultery—instead of these scruples!".

The crushing weight of perfect obedience to God's commands fell squarely on his shoulders. The cross was a necessary condition for his salvation, but it was not sufficient. His brain insisted there was more he *must* do.

He writes, "I was a good monk, and I kept the rules of my order so strictly that I may say that if ever a monk got to heaven by his monkery it was I. All my brothers in the monastery who knew me will bear me out. If I had kept on any longer, I should have killed myself with vigils, prayers, reading, and other work."

And in his commentary on Galatians:

> "Hereby it appears that the doctrine of the gospel (which of all others is most sweet and full of most singular consolation) speaks nothing of our works or of the works of the law, but of the inscrutable mercy and love of God towards most wretched and miserable sinners. Our most merciful Father, seeing us to be oppressed and overwhelmed with the curse of the law, and that we could never be delivered from it of our own power, sent His only Son into the world and laid upon Him all the sins of all men, saying, be Thou Peter that denier; Paul that persecutor and cruel oppressor; David that adulterer; that sinner who did eat the fruit in Eden; that thief who hanged upon the cross, and be Thou that person who has committed the sins of all me; see therefore, that Thou pay and satisfy for them."

His words should remind us of another who realized his attempts at righteous living would not purchase a saving grace,

"If anyone else thinks he has reason for confidence in the flesh, I have more: circumcised on the eighth day, of the people of Israel, of the tribe of Benjamin, a Hebrew of Hebrews; as to the law, a Pharisee; as to zeal, a persecutor of the church; as to righteousness under the law, blameless. But whatever gain I had, I counted as loss for the sake of Christ. Indeed, I count everything as loss because of the surpassing worth of knowing Christ Jesus my Lord. For his sake I have suffered the loss of all things and count them as rubbish, in order that I may gain Christ and be found in him, not having a righteousness of my own that comes from the law, but that which comes through faith in Christ, the righteousness from God that depends on faith—" (Philippians 3:4b-9).

Luther experienced a profound change that would shake not only his own belief system but the world. He realized his ultimate powerlessness to effect his own salvation through any work of his own. We read the impact of this thinking in another stanza of his cherished hymn:

> **With might of our can naught be done,**
> Soon our loss effected;
> **But for us fights** the valiant One,
> Whom God Himself elected.

Ask ye, Who is this?
Jesus Christ it is,
Of Sabaoth Lord,
And there's none other God;
He holds the field forever.

He writes that "might of our" efforts to win the battle against sin and evil, result in "naught", that someone else "for us fights" and this someone is not powerless as we are, but instead, "valiant". He concludes that "there's none other", including himself, who can affect his saving grace.

I propose that the spark that lit the Reformation was, by God's good providence, formed in the kindling of Luther's deep struggle with intrusive and obsessional thoughts and his realization of the fruitlessness of the compulsions he sought to perform to alleviate his distress.

Over a century later, another notable Christian would struggle with scrupulosity. Though he had no formal education of his own, John Bunyan would write the most widely read and culturally impactful book, second only to the Bible, *The Pilgrim's Progress*. Like the main character of his novel, Bunyan would walk the narrow and trial-filled road of the Christian. He writes of intrusive blasphemous thoughts:

"These things may seem ridiculous to others, even as ridiculous as they were in themselves, but to me they were the most tormenting cogitations; Every one of them augmented my misery."

Later, he says,

"For about the space of a month after, a very great storm came down upon me, which handled me twenty times worse than all I had met with before; it came stealing upon me, now by one piece, then by another; first, all my comfort was taken from me, then darkness seized upon me, after which whole floods of blasphemies, both against God, Christ, and the Scriptures, were poured upon my spirit, to my great confusion and astonishment. These blasphemous thoughts were such as also stirred up questions in me, against the very being of God, and of His only beloved Son; as whether there were, in truth, a God, or Christ, or no? And whether the holy

Scriptures were not rather a fable, and cunning story, than the holy and pure word of God?"

Again,

"Sometimes it would run in my thoughts, not so little as a hundred times together…But to be brief, one morning, as I did lie in my bed, I was, as at other times, most fiercely assaulted with this temptation, to sell and part with Christ; the wicked suggestion still running in my mind, 'Sell Him, sell Him, sell Him, sell Him,' as fast as a man could speak. Against which also, in my mind, as at other times, I answered, 'No, no, not for thousands, thousands, thousands,' at least twenty times together. But at last, after much striving, even until I was almost out of breath, I felt this thought pass through my heart, Let Him go, if He will! And I thought also, that I felt my heart desperately consent thereto."

Bunyan's attempts to rid himself of these thoughts through compulsive or ritualistic prayers did not rid him of the assaults. Instead, he writes of a similar realization to Luther,

"One day, as I was passing into the field, suddenly this sentence fell upon my soul: 'Thy righteousness is in heaven.' And I thought that I could see Jesus Christ at God's right hand. Yes, there indeed was my righteousness, so that wherever I was, or whatever I was doing, God could not say about me that I did not have righteousness, for it was standing there before Him."

Bunyan fell headlong into his inability to affect his own righteousness before God. It wasn't caused by him or held by him and couldn't be changed by him, as that Righteousness was Christ "standing there before Him".

In my office, you will find Calvin's *Institutes of the Christian Religion*, *The Westminster Confession of Faith and Catechisms*, and *The Heidelberg Catechism* among other foundational texts of the Reformation. I think of how these works proclaim both our profound unworthiness and inability to affect saving grace alongside God's immeasurable, irresistible call. I see the freedom this produces for the sufferer with OCD. Praise God that through the pain Luther, Bunyan, and many others experienced, they received the blessing of being washed in a certainty, not in self, but in God's power to save, and that they chose to share this Biblical theology with the world.

Appendix 4 – The Role of the Church

One of the first places a Christian struggling with OCD that has not yet been diagnosed presents is to the church. The reason for this may be related to their distress (broadly) or to elements of scrupulosity (more specifically). This is what makes a clear understanding of OCD and its presentation all the more important for pastors, elders, and lay counselors. A patient presenting with intrusive thoughts of committing a sin or blaspheming God can mistakenly be counseled by a well-intentioned pastor to "pray more". Similarly, someone who rereads passages of scripture repeatedly to ensure they have a "perfect understanding" may prompt an elder to initiate a lengthy discussion of related theological material. Given what we have discussed earlier in the journal, freedom from OCD comes not as we indulge the compulsions that our brains have become convinced are necessary to experience peace, but in resisting those same compulsions and seeing that the feared event has not occurred. For the patient with OCD, this is a great act of faith, one that glorifies God.

A strong relationship with the church leaders who care for a particular patient is of great clinical importance. Together, the clinician and the pastor can work towards healing. For more information on an Integrated Christian Psychiatry approach, see my book, *The Mind for His Glory: A philosophy of applied Christian psychiatry.*

Appendix 5 – PANDAS

One of the most common questions I am asked by parents is, "Is there a cause for OCD?" Current theory is that OCD results from a variety of factors, both genetic and environmental. One area of interest, however, is the potential role of *Streptococcal* infections in childhood (which are especially common as strep throat, or more infrequently, Scarlet Fever) in potentially causing OCD symptoms. The syndrome has been named Pediatric

Autoimmune Neuropsychiatric Disorders Associated with *Streptococcal* Infections (PANDAS).

It is thought that *Streptococcal* bacteria have evolved over time to evade detection by our immune system, adopting characteristics similar to those of normal human tissues (found in the heart, skin, brain, etc.). Eventually, the body's immune system recognizes the foreign invaders and develops antibodies against them. These antibodies then flag both *Streptococcal* bacteria and the normal human tissues they were mimicking for destruction. It is thought that this misdirected immune activity leads to damage in the regions of the brain that lead to OCD. PANDAS generally presents as a sudden, almost overnight, emergence of OCD and/or tic-like behavior in a child following a strep infection. PANDAS can impact children generally from around age 3 to adolescence. It is not known if adolescents or adults could develop immune-mediated OCD.

Treatment of PANDAS starts with adequate treatment of any remaining strep infection, usually with antibiotics. Neuropsychiatric symptoms such as OCD and tics can be treated as they would in any other child, generally through the treatments discussed in the early chapters of this journal.

PANDAS research continues but what it has shown us so far is that OCD and other mental health conditions are multifactorial and can include both physical and nonphysical, genetic and environmental factors.

Appendix 6 – Co-Occurring and Related Disorders

There are several frequently co-occurring conditions that may exist alongside OCD. Patients with OCD may also experience major depressive episodes, other anxiety disorders, phobias, or personality disorders. It is important for patients suspected of having OCD to have a full assessment, as treating these co-occurring disorders will be important for overall mental health.

The *DSM* lists several disorders that are related to OCD due to increasing evidence that they share similar pathophysiology. They include: "body dysmorphic disorder, hoarding disorder, trichotillomania (hairpulling disorder), excoriation (skin-picking) disorder, substance/medication-induced obsessive-compulsive and related disorder, obsessive-compulsive and related disorder due to another medical condition, and other specified obsessive-compulsive and related disorder and unspecified obsessive-compulsive and related disorder (e.g., body-focused repetitive behavior disorder, obsessional jealousy)." Our understanding of how OCD functions as both a heightened sense that something is "wrong" and inordinate value assigned to particular actions aimed at righting that wrong begins to make clear the associations between the above disorders (excepting substance-medication induced OCD and OCD due to another medical condition which have different etiologies but may share a similar presentation).

Body Dysmorphic Disorder – Patients struggling with Body Dysmorphic Disorder have a perceived flaw in their appearance that is minimal or absent when viewed from an outsider's perspective. They may feel compelled to groom, assess, or weigh themselves among other rituals, which are aimed at reducing the distress caused by this perceived flaw.

Hoarding Disorder – Patients who struggle with hoarding disorder are unable to discard objects of little to no value to such an extreme degree that it inhibits their functioning. Initially, the link between Hoarding Disorder and OCD may not seem apparent, but when we consider that OCD has a lot to do with assigning value (to the usefulness of particular behaviors), the links to Hoarding Disorder begin to appear. Take a handwashing compulsion; washing your hands after a long day is of great value and is good practice. But how helpful is it to wash your hands the 15th time? The problem in OCD is that the value assigned to that action is just as prominent the 15th time as the first time. It's, in part, a problem with overvaluing. In Hoarding Disorder, not only is the value of worthless objects increased, but the fear regarding something bad happening if objects are discarded mirrors the feared consequence of not performing a compulsion in OCD.

Trichotillomania and Excoriation Disorder – Trichotillomania stands for hair pulling, and excoriation is skin picking. Many patients with OCD also struggle with one or both of these conditions. They are related to OCD in part because of the inability to inhibit signals coming from the deep brain that tell the person to pick or pull at skin or hair.

Tic Disorder – Tic disorder can involve both movements and/or vocalizations and is commonly seen alongside OCD.

Appendix 7 – One of OCD's Last Stands

I wanted to take a moment to talk about a particular intrusive thought I've seen creep into patients' minds, especially toward the end of treatment. After many of the subtypes of OCD have been addressed, there arises an intrusive thought, "What if it wasn't OCD all along?". The intrusive thought attempts to convince a patient that, despite all the evidence we have seen that OCD has been present, despite all the success in resisting intrusive thoughts and compulsions, it wasn't OCD after all. I've called this OCD's Last Stand. Not all patients experience it, but it is a common occurrence.

The corresponding compulsion that usually accompanies the intrusive thought is a reassurance seeking from me or other clinicians, a textbook, online resources, etc. A patient may request to review early visit notes, diagnostic criteria, and testing, etc. It remains an attempt to resolve a perception of uncertainty.

Patients may grow frustrated when I (as their treating clinician) don't reassure them repeatedly that "this is all OCD". If I were to continually reassure patients that "this is all OCD", I would be participating in and strengthening the very loop that is keeping them in bondage. By refusing to participate in the loop, we work for the patient's healing.

Appendix 8 – Family and Friends

The reassurance seeking from patients toward their clinicians is not limited to the medical setting. This is also true of loved ones. Family members, friends, pastors, and other care team members can all find themselves as a part of an OCD loop. Though it's difficult to see someone we care for in pain, the right thing to do is not to participate in a patient's compulsion. This can still be done in love, however. I recommend a gentle reminder: "I care for you, but I'm not going to participate in an OCD loop". If that phrase itself becomes a compulsive thought, simply responding with "No, I'm sorry" or "No" may be appropriate. There is much more that could be said to you, family and friends. Suffice it to say, for now, your care for your loved one, even in reading this journal, is a true gift. It's a quiet presence that says you are not alone. What we attempt to give imperfectly, Jesus gives perfectly, and he has ordained that an extension of his healing hand would come through you as you walk and sit alongside someone in suffering.

Appendix 9 – Other Patients' Experiences

We read in 2 Corinthians, "Blessed be the God and Father of our Lord Jesus Christ, the Father of mercies and God of all comfort, who comforts us in all our affliction, so that we may be able to comfort those who are in any affliction, with the comfort with which we ourselves are comforted by God" (2 Corinthians 1:3-4).

I've asked real patients what message they might like to deliver to someone who suffers, as they did/do, with OCD. Here are their words that you might know you are not alone, and be encouraged:

* * *

I had been struggling with OCD long before my clinician ever named it for me. I always thought it was just anxiety or Christian moralism, but they correctly diagnosed it as scrupulosity OCD. Upon being officially diagnosed with OCD, I felt extremely defeated, sad, and like an oddball. I didn't want to be the OCD guy. However, as we began to work through ERP, as painful as it felt in the moment, so many things began to click. It wasn't a magic bullet, but I felt a sense of confidence now that my Goliath had a name. I didn't want to lean into the diagnosis and make it my identity, but after reading a book about Martin Luther's scrupulosity OCD, I didn't feel so isolated or odd anymore. It took immense trust in the therapeutic process, but with time, therapy, and the sanctifying work of the Holy Spirit, I no longer gave my scrupulous thoughts as much credence as I once did. I would think to my scrupulous thoughts, "You are OCD, and although you seem scary, I'm choosing to ignore you."

If you are walking through scrupulosity OCD, or any type of OCD for that matter, just remember, the journey towards healing and wholeness is NOT linear. Even though I am in a much better place with my OCD than when I first began addressing my OCD (which at the beginning of my journey I never thought I could be where I am now), I still have my days. Sometimes they are more weeks than days to be honest. But that is all part of the journey. Like Hebrews says, we do not have a high priest who is unable to sympathize with our weaknesses (Hebrews 4:15). Jesus understands your OCD more than you do, He will never leave you, and we look forward to eternity with him when every sickness and disease is erased. But until then, we fight the good fight, knowing the battle belongs to the Lord.

* * *

OCD felt like it came out of nowhere for me in college. It began to manifest during the COVID era when I went from being busy all the time to having a lot of free time. I feel this is what triggered my OCD. I have always dealt with minor OCD struggles from childhood, such as: completing homework assignments perfectly, dealing with the "what if" thought of my dad dying when he left for work, checking locks, etc. It wasn't until college that OCD started to attack me morally and as who I am in Christ. This led to many sleepless nights as I tried to navigate why my brain was locked on intrusive thoughts that made my skin crawl. The summer before I graduated from college, I decided to get help from a counselor, but it wasn't until I was married and moved to the DC area that a friend from church connected me with a Christian psychiatry practice. His ability to help me understand exposure therapy as it aligns with God's Word was the biggest change for me. Over the journey of a year, I slowly began to see my Father in Heaven as loving me and not being mad at me. That was the biggest help. Today, I am able to walk through life as if I don't have OCD, which I never thought would be the case. It didn't happen on my timetable, but the process was worth it. I still have my moments where the "what if" thoughts come in, but my time spiraling over them has decreased significantly. It is such a gift to be able to live life in the present, and I am very thankful to Adam and his practice for helping me get to where I am today. Ultimately, I praise God for his grace and love and the tools he has given me to help me live freely in Christ and not in fear.

* * *

For me, symptoms of OCD began in late middle school and early high school, though looking back, there were minor signs from early childhood. There were several themes that I struggled with, from intrusive thoughts of same-sex attraction to fears about salvation, and through the years, the "topic" of

OCD has shifted. Before the diagnosis was made, I thought I was losing my mind. Every intrusive thought felt like absolute truth, so I would go to battle in prayer or with other coping mechanisms. I must have asked Jesus into my heart a thousand times, constantly worrying I didn't "believe enough" or didn't "want it enough".

I resisted seeking professional help for what I was experiencing for a while. Finally, my family sat me down and essentially said it was no longer an option. I was angry with them at the time, but reluctantly agreed. As I looked at the list of potential obsessions and compulsions, I was amazed. The number of things I checked off on that list was shocking. Things I thought only I experienced were there in black and white on the page. Others experienced this too. By the time the psychologist delivered the diagnosis, I was no longer surprised. In fact, there was a deep relief.

I started both a medication as well as began a formal ERP process. We didn't find the right fit with the first medication, but the second one was night and day. I was surprised because after the first medication didn't work, I had low expectations for the second, but wow. It also didn't do everything I needed; ERP was important, too.

ERP was very difficult. It meant entering the darkest places and trusting that God would still protect me from the things I feared, even though I didn't give in to the compulsions. In time, I was able to pray in freedom, not out of a compulsion.

I look back now and see the early years with OCD as very painful and challenging, but I also see God's goodness toward me in and through it. I believe there's a strength that has come through struggling with OCD. When trials come now, I look back and say to my savior, "We made it through that, we can make it through this."

I still struggle with obsessions and compulsions on occasion, and there have been periods of my life where I have been on or off medication, but ultimately, things have been on a positive trajectory. Don't lose hope if you find yourself in a similar place to me. Grab hold of the good gifts God has given in science, medicine, and psychology, and know that he will bring you successfully through whatever he brings you to.

* * *

Appendix 10 — Other Resources

Emlet M. Scrupulosity: When Doubts Devour. *JBC.* 2019;33(3):11-40.

Faith & Medicine Foundation - https://www.faithandmedicine.foundation/

Dr. Ian Osborn, MD - https://ocdandchristianity.com/ian-osborn-md/

International OCD Foundation - https://www.iocdf.org/

NOCD - https://www.treatmyocd.com/

References

1. Goodman WK, Storch EA, Sheth SA. Harmonizing the Neurobiology and Treatment of

Obsessive-Compulsive Disorder. AJP. 2021;178(1):17-29.

doi:10.1176/appi.ajp.2020.20111601

2. Seyedmirzaei H, Bayan N, Ohadi MAD, Cattarinussi G, Sambataro F. Effects of antidepressants on brain structure and function in patients with obsessive-compulsive disorder: A review of neuroimaging studies. Psychiatry Research: Neuroimaging.

2024;342:111842. doi:10.1016/j.pscychresns.2024.111842

3. Obsession and Compulsion Checklist adapted and Modified from Freedom From Obsessive

Compulsive Disorder: A Personalized Recovery Program for Living with Uncertainty by Jonathan Grayson.

4. Goodman WK, Price LH, Rasmussen SA, et al. Yale-Brown Obsessive Compulsive Scale.

Published online April 10, 2017. doi:10.1037/t57982-000

5. Luther M. Commentary on Galatians. Digireads.com; 2019.

6. Osborn I. Martin Luther's Obsessive-Compulsive Disorder: How the Great Reformer Cured OCD and

What He Learned. OCD Resources Publishing; 2023.

7. Bainton RH. Here I Stand: A Life of Martin Luther. Reprint edition. Abingdon Press; 2013.

8. Bunyan J. Grace Abounding to the Chief of Sinners - Updated Edition. (Miller P, ed.). Aneko Press;

2017.

9. PANDAS—Questions and Answers - National Institute of Mental Health (NIMH).

Accessed May 7, 2025. https://www.nimh.nih.gov/health/publications/pandas

Made in the USA
Middletown, DE
19 November 2025

21065117R00053